AF583751

OUR STREETS

THE REGIONAL CITIES & MAJOR TOWNS PROJECT

Joyce Evans, *House, Princes Street*, Burnie, Tasmania

FOREWORD

I spent the 1990s at university (for longer than I should have), playing in bands, doing some very ordinary acting, standing on stage with a microphone and, finally, presenting the Drive show for the ABC on Triple J. Many of these endeavours saw me hitting the road to perform in or broadcast from regional cities and towns. These experiences helped me connect with people and places far away from my various capital city enclaves.

A flick through the pages of this book or the list of towns represented reads like a gig guide from the past for me. It could have been me getting out of those now-ancient cars in any one of those glorious main streets.

In Ballarat, after a gig at a well-known rock and roll establishment, we found ourselves sleeping in the living room of complete strangers after discovering that the accommodation upstairs at the pub was riddled with bedbugs.

In far-flung Albany, I dined on some of the best Thai food in the country after failing to excite a lacklustre crowd at the local theatre on a Saturday night, competing unsuccessfully with a 21st birthday at the footy club.

Much further north in Kalgoorlie, in the local ABC building, I broadcast from a 1950s-era radio panel, sending the Triple J music out in mono, potentially for the very first and last time.

In Wagga Wagga, I walked the main street, passing a full-to-the-brim video store, looking for somewhere decent to eat, only to find myself dining at a pizza restaurant that had run out of cheese.

Up the road in Goulburn, I still remember eating Chinese food with a fork and spoon and watching guys in Holden Monaros and Ford Coupes do laps up and down the main drag.

In Newcastle, we rolled around town with a handycam making a terrible little film, but soaked up the layers of history and witnessed the start of the slow transformation of a city breaking away from some of its industrial past.

With my mum in the passenger seat, we saw the house in Bendigo where my grandmother grew up, and watched the tram go by, a glorious and everlasting reminder of the almighty power of the gold rush.

In the New South Wales–Victoria border town of Echuca, my mates walked over the bridge to play the pokies while I stumped up the courage to ring a girl from university who had returned home to Echuca for the holidays. She didn't answer.

In Geelong, where you couldn't miss the Ford signs, I drank a few pots at the pub opposite Kardinia Park and then watched the Cats beat Richmond before driving back to Melbourne with a grin on my face.

Up north in the Queensland town of Maryborough, we slept overnight outside the mechanic's while we waited for a part to come up from Brisbane. The publican didn't care much for my ponytail, and I was relieved when the part arrived and we were able to leave.

On another road trip, going fishing with some mates, we had a hankering for a vanilla slice. A bakery in Tumut in southern New South Wales more than did the trick; in fact, I vividly remember going back for a second.

In Renmark, South Australia, I broadcast by the side of the Murray, the summer breeze skimming the famous brown water and rustling the leaves of the weeping willow. After the broadcast, we chatted with a fifteen-year-old kid who had walked ten kilometres into town to see his station go to air. After we packed up, we drove past him on the highway and gave him a lift home. He was so excited he dragged his mum out to meet us.

Our built heritage connects us to our memories, and our interactions—no matter how small or varied—bind us to place and country. The continued documentation of streets is vitally important, and although the 1990s seem like a minute ago to many, a quick check of the calculator proves that to be untrue. The varied architecture, some good, some bad, tells the story of us and that's all we have.

I hope these images can remind you of connections. Even if the vignettes may not be of places you have visited, they may conjure up memories of something similar. In times where division prospers, small moments that unite us are more important than ever.

Tim Ross

OUR STREETS

In the mid-1990s, the National Library commissioned around 18 photographers to photograph the buildings of 90 regional cities and country towns Australia wide.

The project was created to 'acquire photographs of a selection of towns for which contemporary photography is lacking … [and] add to holdings of photographs of towns for which we hold no recent photographs, and in some cases, few photographs at all'. Capital cities were not part of the project as there were sufficient records of those places in the Library's collection and in the collections of other institutions. In each town, the photographers were instructed to capture the following: streets; buildings, including banks and post offices; railway stations; monuments, including war memorials; houses; parks and gardens; swimming pools; playing fields; sporting activities; schools; motels; social life; industry; factories; civic, religious and military functions; lakes, river and beaches; and other natural features. They were told not to include advertising signs or street signs, unless in a wider context, nor close-up shots of owners of shops and businesses. Around 2,600 images were generated and absorbed into the Library's collection, forming a valuable record of the range of buildings that existed in these towns and regional cities at that time.

Today, we are familiar with the dramatic, stylised shots of buildings found in coffee table books on contemporary architecture, in the latest architecture and design magazines or in the marketing collateral of real estate agencies and architecture firms. These images are usually captured by digital cameras, the colours are highly saturated, there are close-ups of interesting design details, and the buildings are shot from angles and in light to show them to their best advantage.

The images in the Regional Cities and Major Towns project are quite different. Here we have front-on portraits, captured on real film, in black and white. The photographers were creating documentary records, not high art, and they approached the subject matter democratically, including commonplace buildings as well as architecturally significant ones in austere, clinical images. For the sake of pragmatism, the photographers used a uniform approach; there are no tricks here to make the buildings more engaging than they already are. The buildings are captured from a respectful distance, allowing us to make as objective a comparison as possible between them.

What results is an excellent photographic typology of the streets and buildings of regional Australia in the 1990s. Captured, too, is a history of regional Australia. The buildings photographed show a tale of two centuries, beginning with foundation and incredible growth. Most Australian towns, and the majority of the 90 captured in the Regional Cities and Major Towns project, were established in the nineteenth century, when rural areas produced the majority of Australia's wealth, primarily through wool, wheat and gold, and other mined minerals. Growth was facilitated by the establishment of rail networks in the 1850s bridging vast distances, connecting towns with towns, as well as cities and the coast. Some of the oldest buildings captured by the photographers are train stations built during the nineteenth-century railway boom. They range from the humble timber station (p21) at Wycheproof, Victoria, with its small architectural embellishments like the decorated capitals at the top of the verandah posts, to the much grander Beaux Arts-style station (p19) at Ballarat, a symmetrical, spectacular grab bag of classically inspired flourishes, signifying that you had arrived in one of the towns that built Victoria's wealth.

In the twentieth century, few new Australian towns were established. Instead, the story is one of migration from those established towns in the bush to those by the sea. At Federation in 1901, 61% of Australians lived in country areas, 32% in capital cities and 7% in coastal towns. One hundred years later, the landscape had changed substantially: with 64% of Australians living in capital cities, 19% in coastal towns and cities, and only 17% in country areas. Shifting trends in Australian agriculture, including greater mechanisation of farm equipment, fly-in-fly-out miners who don't settle in the towns next to where they work and the closure of large manufacturing plants in regional Australia

RIGHT: Marianne Irvine, *Old railway station building*, Wycheproof, Victoria, 1995
OPPOSITE: Brendan Bell, *Shopping mall*, Dubbo, New South Wales, 1994

have contributed to this change. Shops and services that supported small communities closed, partly because of the population shift but also because goods and services in the new postwar shopping malls of larger regional centres, replete with cookie-cutter chain stores, were cheaper than on main street. One example is the city centre shopping mall (p106) in Dubbo, New South Wales, which, in the spirit of postmodernism, welcomes shoppers by borrowing design features from earlier ages, such as an Art Deco-style font and a fanlight window.

While these trends had changed the fabric of many regional towns by the 1990s, so too did the continued postwar growth in tourism. A large part of the charm of Australian towns for visitors lay in the relatively untouched nature of the built environment. Economic stagnation and population redistribution meant that there had been far less need for the tear-down/build-something-new cycle of the capital cities. As a result, there was (and still is) a higher proportion of older buildings in country towns. Contributing to the preservation of country Australia's heritage was the rise of the building conservation movement, which began with the formation of the National Trusts in Australia from the 1940s, peaking after the Green Bans in the 1970s, when builders and labourers refused to work on the demolition of buildings for environmental and social reasons. This increased awareness of the importance of preserving Australian buildings and provided the movement with the bureaucratic voice and tools to save them.

Today, one of the great attractions of touring regional Australia is these preserved buildings. Tourists love the charming and the old: the tea house, the small church sitting in a quiet churchyard. Small villages and towns like Berrima in New South Wales and Burra in South Australia attract tourists to their collection of picturesque nineteenth-century stone buildings and experiences that exploit their attractiveness. There are also buildings in country towns that rival the grand historic architecture of capital cities—and, arguably, they are more imposing in the urban landscape of a country town. In the wake of the gold rushes, a raft of impressive public buildings sprang up in Australian towns and cities. Goulburn's fine courthouse (p50), designed by colonial architect James Barnet and built between 1885 and 1887, is a Victorian Free Classical

building equal to many grand courthouses in the capital cities. In a country town like Goulburn, New South Wales, it stands out more by virtue of its size in relation to the rest of the architecture in the town. The West Australian gold rushes of the 1890s saw a proliferation of ornate, dominating public buildings. York Hotel (p139) in Hannan Street, Kalgoorlie, had its foundation stone laid in 1900. Its architectural style is Federation Anglo-Dutch but it is best described as 'bombastic'. The way these buildings occupy space is little different now to when they were constructed. Unlike in the cities, there are fewer apartment blocks or curtain-walled multistorey office buildings being built to challenge their dominance of the skyline.

Something not captured in these photos from the 1990s is the way buildings have been revitalised by the continued growth of arts, food and wine tourism, and the movement of tree- and sea-changers away from capital cities, especially since COVID. A contemporary viewer brings this knowledge to the pictures and sees the seeds for revitalisation and regrowth alongside the nostalgia and occasional decay. In 1995, the Art Deco Paragon movie theatre (p143) in Queenstown, Tasmania, was living a second life as an indoor cricket centre. Since then, Queenstown has repositioned itself as a tourist gateway to the unique wonders of the Tasmanian Southwest, and the Paragon has been restored as a cinema and music venue.

A perennial tourist attraction, both then and now, is kitsch. One of the great regional Australian contributions to this aspect of the built environment has been 'Big Things', which began to appear around the country in the latter part of the twentieth century. Structures like the Giant Pineapple (p34) in Gympie, Queensland, and the Big Crocodile (p35) in Wyndham, Western Australia, operate in a strange space between novelty architecture and sculpture, and are celebrations of local culture or industry. The Gympie big pineapple was demolished in 2008, but never fear pineapple fans: there is another, one hour's drive away in Woombye.

Big Things may stand out in a country town but their architectural significance is up for debate. They were photographed because they contribute to the character of a town. So many of the buildings here fall into this category. They are the everyday buildings found in country towns, the ones which tell a story but are not necessarily the finest example of their style—or perhaps don't have any recognisable style at all. Some may still be important for social or historical reasons, such as the Lee Tong store (p96) in Port Wyndham, Western Australia, which illustrates a utilitarian, make-it-with-whatever-comes-to-hand approach to building, but is significant because of how it connects to the broader story of Australian-Chinese history and mining towns in the nineteenth century. Even when the importance of their stories is not as apparent, the houses and local shops of Australia's towns are a connective tissue between the architectural highlights, and are part of what gives a place its identity.

It is this element that makes the project, and this book, particularly fascinating. Revisiting the images almost three decades after they were taken, they speak in ways quite distinct from the specificity of their role in the history of a particular town or the architectural development of its built environment. This is to do with personal experience, with memory. It's what we bring to the pictures of these buildings, whether they are everyday or extraordinary. If you didn't grow up in one of these towns, there's a good chance you at least visited, drove through, stopped at or holidayed in one. These streets were important stages for big and small events in our lives. This collection encourages us to play 'spot the building, street or town'. Your family used to visit such and such a place during the school holidays. You particularly remember that post office, or that swimming pool or that main street. The shops now may have different tenants, but the bakery is still there. Or perhaps you still live there, but that building has been demolished. Even the buildings we've never seen feel familiar. You've never driven down that street or stood outside that house or that post office, but they are so representative that they conjure up other streets, houses or post offices that you do know.

Our Streets presents a small selection of the 2,600 photographs produced during the Regional Cities and Major Towns project. It is organised by building type rather than location as this allows us to tease out the similarities and differences between towns and buildings. There is a huge variety of architectural styles here, influenced by the period of construction, the fortunes of the town, as well as their locations and climate—there is a reason you don't see many Queenslanders in Tasmania or surf clubs in outback Western Australia. But there are also amazing similarities between towns and the buildings that make them, highlighting why we seem to uncannily recognise places and buildings we haven't been to. It's this collective memory of the towns and their buildings that binds us as Australians.

Matthew Jones
National Library of Australia

Photographs from the Regional Cities and Major Towns project were displayed in the Australian Dreams: Picturing Our Built World exhibition, which showed at the National Library of Australia in 2020–2021.

OPPOSITE: Mike Key, *Paragon theatre, McNamara Street*, Queenstown, Tasmania, 1995
ABOVE: Reg Alder, *Lee Tong store*, Port Wyndham, Western Australia, 1994

COMING & GOING

We can travel vast distances in Australia passing very few signs of a built environment. The approach to a country town, whether by road or rail, might seem unremarkable, depending on how familiar we are with the landscape and how far we've come, but it signposts the sort of place and community we are about to encounter. There might be signs of heavy and light industry—flour mills, silos, car yards and mechanics—as well as petrol stations, train stations, Big Things, motels and other markers of human activity. There can be visual poetry to the grand siding buildings or the sugar terminal rearing up from flat country. But many of these structures on the outskirts of Australia's towns are purpose-built spaces performing a specific function.

There is real beauty, though, in our main streets. It is here we see the telltale signs of when a particular town had its heyday, when its important public buildings were designed and erected, how old buildings have been repurposed or maintained, and what is important to the residents of the town. As we come and go along the main commercial strip, catch a train or drive out of town, these are the buildings we see.

Brendan Bell, *Bulk grains terminal*, Port Lincoln, South Australia, 1997

John Werrett, *Yallourn 'W' power station*, Yallourn, Victoria, 1994

Gordon Undy, *Bulk sugar terminal*, Mackay, Queensland, 1995

Mike Key, *Gasworks*, Launceston, Tasmania, 1995

Fiona MacDonald Brand, *Keys Excelsior flour mills*, Narrabri, New South Wales, 1994

Robert Deane, *Railway siding buildings, Old Tooth maltings*, Mittagong, New South Wales, 1996

Raymond De Berquelle, *Old port from the Murray River bank*, Echuca, Victoria, 1994

Grant Ellmers, *Railway station, Lydiard Street North*, Ballarat, Victoria, 1994

Bob Miller, *Railway station*, Alice Springs, Northern Territory, 1994

Marianne Irvine, *Old railway station building*, Wycheproof, Victoria, 1995

POST
THRIFT
COFFEE LOUNGE
HARDWARE
OPEN
7 DAYS

Bob Miller, *Hutchison Street*, Coober Pedy, South Australia, 1994

Mike Key, *Orr Street*, Queenstown, Tasmania, 1995

Bob Miller, *Car parts and service centre*, Katherine, Northern Territory, 1996

Brendan Bell, *Garage*, Bega, New South Wales, 1994

Gordon Undy, *Herbert Street*, Bowen, Queensland, 1995

Peter Mathew, *Murray Street*, Gawler, South Australia, 1995

Joyce Evans, *McLachlan Street*, Horsham, Victoria, 1995

Aaron Bunch, *Victoria Street*, Bunbury, Western Australia, 1995

Mike Key, *Tamar Street*, Launceston, Tasmania, 1995

Aaron Bunch, *Spencer Street*, Albany, Western Australia, 1995

Aaron Bunch, *Blair Street*, Bunbury, Western Australia, 1995

Bob Miller, *The Big Golden Guitar*, Tamworth, New South Wales, 1995

Autogas
UNLEADED
63.9
SUPER
65.9
CA

Reg Alder, *The Big Crocodile*, Wyndham, Western Australia, 1994

Glenn Rees, *The Giant Pineapple*, Gympie, Queensland, 1995

TAKING CARE OF BUSINESS

Some of our most interesting buildings are those we wouldn't necessarily choose to spend time in. Imposing nineteenth-century banks, post offices, courthouses and town halls are familiar sights from Launceston to Townsville, often built in the Victorian or Federation periods when these buildings were central to daily life. Usually multi-storied, with grand facades, arches, columns or porticos, they can appear incongruous alongside main street's utilitarian office spaces and shops erected in the second half of the twentieth century. Fortunately for us, their grandeur is sometimes preserved and they are set back within landscaped gardens or bricked courtyards.

Less imposing but no less attractive are the civic buildings built post-Federation. Shepparton's Art Deco courthouse (p49) today is dwarfed by grand, new law courts, but its curves, geometry and squat sturdiness have born witness to a hundred years of Shepparton history. Tumut's old council chambers (p47), established around the creation of Tumut Shire in 1928, have the same geometric shapes and simple, clean design. Built just before the electricity current from neighbouring Burrinjuck was extended to Tumut—and a decade before the sewerage system was installed—the building was erected during a period of change and development. By the 1990s, many of these buildings were being used as multi-purpose spaces, with community groups and local businesses as tenants.

Raymond de Berquelle, *Bank of NSW, High Street*, Echuca, Victoria, 1994

Brendon Kelson, *ANZ bank, Parker Street*, Cootamundra, New South Wales, 1996

Joyce Evans, *National bank*, Gundagai, New South Wales, 1994

LAUNCESTON POST OFFICE
CZ-7082

Fiona MacDonald Brand, *Post office, Maitland Street*, Narrabri, New South Wales, 1994

Mike Key, *Post office, Cameron Street*, Launceston, Tasmania, 1995

Brendan Bell, *Post office*, Whyalla, South Australia, 1997

Bob Miller, *Post office*, Hermannsburg, Northern Territory, 1994

Gordon Undy, *Customs house, cnr The Strand and Wickham Street*, Townsville, Queensland, 1995

Aaron Bunch, *Town hall*, Albany, Western Australia, 1995

Gordon Undy, *Council chambers, Abbott Street*, Cairns, Queensland, 1995

Brendon Kelson, *Council chambers, Capper Street*, Tumut, New South Wales, 1996

Joyce Evans, *State government offices, cnr Fenwick and Little Malop streets*, Geelong, Victoria, 1996

Raymond de Berquelle, *Court house, High Street*, Shepparton, Victoria, 1994

Joyce Evans, *Court house, Montague Street*, Goulburn, New South Wales, 1994

Aaron Bunch, *Court house*, Bunbury, Western Australia, 1995

Aaron Bunch, *Court house*, Boulder, Western Australia, 1995

Joyce Evans, *Police station*, Burnie, Tasmania, 1995

Brendan Bell, *Police station*, Port Lincoln, South Australia, 1997

Police

Grant Ellmers, *Fire station, Kiewa Street*, Albury, New South Wales, 1994

Bob Miller, *Fire station, Molesworth Street*, Lismore, New South Wales, 1995

Gordon Undy, *Ambulance*, Charters Towers, Queensland, 1996

Gordon Undy, *Hospital*, Charters Towers, Queensland, 1996

Aaron Bunch, *Regional hospital*, Geraldton, Western Australia, 1995

Grant Ellmers, *St John of God hospital, Drummond Street*, Ballarat, Victoria, 1994

BUILDING COMMUNITY

People are mostly missing from the photographs of the Regional Cities and Major Towns project, except occasionally as a kind of staffage (accessories in landscape photography, usually to show scale or enliven a scene). But it is the communities that have grown up in these towns that give them their unique character, however similar (or not) the buildings might appear across the country. In this section are places where communities gather or are formed. Many capture the character of a town at a particular time in its history, such as Bendigo's Chinese Association building (p72) or Hamilton's Masonic temple (p73), while others represent an enduring shared experience, such as Charters Towers' central school (p68) or Queenstown's Vietnam War memorial (p64).

We gather for countless reasons, including to reflect and worship. The RSL clubs of country Australia remain places where communities get together to have a meal or a beer and, particularly on designated days of remembrance, to reflect on a shared miliary history. While many are huge ritzy buildings erected in the 1980s and 1990s, some venues exude Art Deco charm or mid-century modern design. Churches are among our oldest buildings, and often the best-preserved examples of architectural styles. Two Anglican churches show just how wide the range of styles is: St George's in Gawler (p81) is a Gothic masterpiece of blue stone, sandstone and slate; while Holy Trinity in Moe (p82), transplanted to an open-air museum, is a small weatherboard building with a timber-shingle roof.

Gordon Undy, *RSL club*, Mackay, Queensland, 1995

Mike Key, *Vietnam War memorial*, Queenstown, Tasmania, 1995

Grant Ellmers, *Boer War memorial, Sturt Street*, Ballarat, Victoria, 1994

Brendon Kelson, *Ex-servicemen's club, Wallendoon and Parker streets*, Cootamundra, New South Wales, 1996

Brendan Bell, *Town clock*, Renmark, South Australia, 1997

Gordon Undy, *Central state school*, Charters Towers, Queensland, 1996

Raymond de Berquelle, *Presbyterian school, Campbell Street*, Swan Hill, Victoria, 1994

Brendan Bell, *St Bede's primary school*, Braidwood, New South Wales, 1994

Marianne Irvine, *P12 college*, Wycheproof, Victoria, 1995

John Werrett, *Chinese Association building*, Bendigo, Victoria, 1995

Grant Ellmers, *Masonic temple, Lonsdale Street*, Hamilton, Victoria, 1994

Raymond De Berquelle, *The Salvation Army citadel, High Street*, Echuca, Victoria, 1994

Robert Deane, *Former boys club, Hay Street*, Holbrook, New South Wales, 1996

John Werrett, *Kangaroo Flat YMCA*, Bendigo, Victoria, 1995

Bob Miller, *Workers club, Keen Street*, Lismore, New South Wales, 1995

Gordon Undy, *Church of Christ*, Charters Towers, Queensland, 1996

John Werrett, *Holy Cross Lutheran church*, Murray Bridge, South Australia, 1994

Joyce Evans, *Former synagogue*, Broken Hill, New South Wales, 1996

Peter Mathew, *St George's Anglican church*, Gawler, South Australia, 1995

Jennifer Aitken, *Old Gippstown church*, Moe, Victoria, 1995

Aaron Bunch, *St Patrick's cathedral*, Bunbury, Western Australia, 1995

Glenn Rees, *St John's Lutheran church*, Bundaberg, Queensland, 1995

Raymond De Berquelle, *Mosque, cnr Maple and Acacia streets*, Shepparton, Victoria, 1994

Brendan Bell, *Anglican church and Greek orthodox church*, Port Pirie, South Australia, 1997

John Werrett, *Church of Christ*, Victor Harbor, South Australia, 1995

SHOPPING

Perhaps more than any other, this section is a time capsule of 1990s Australia. Keith's Bakery (p94–95) might no longer exist on Clarendon Street in Derby, but locals and people travelling through the town will have memories of stopping there. Shops are the lifeblood of many regional cities and towns, as places of employment that sustain local communities, as well as places where people see each other on a daily basis.

The buildings that house local businesses often have much longer histories, beginning life as something completely different. Port Pirie's wash-house and laundromat on Florence Street (p99) was once a Lutheran church, a central meeting place for the town's very small Lutheran community before the First World War caused a flare-up of anti-German sentiment. Fosseys (p105) in Charters Towers was originally a grand department store, offering a new style of shopping to genteel, mainly female customers in remote northern Queensland. It was commissioned at the height of the Charters Towers goldfield in 1909 and built of local red bricks, loosely in the style of Federation architecture.

Bob Miller, *General store, Niagara Street*, Armidale, New South Wales, 1994

Jennifer Aitken, *Milk bar, Rubery Street*, Moe, Victoria, 1995

Robert Deane, *Antiques shop, Yass Street*, Gunning, New South Wales, 1995

Joyce Evans, *Pat's drapery next to burned-down supermarket*, Menindee, New South Wales, 1996

Brendon Kelson, *J.D.'s Jam Factory, Grenfell Road*, Young, New South Wales, 1996

PH. DE BY (091) 911.659
KEITH'S
LUN
OPEN

Aaron Bunch, *Keith's bakery, Clarendon Street*, Derby, Western Australia, 1995

Reg Alder, *Lee Tong store*, Port Wyndham, Western Australia, 1994

John Werrett, *Shake 'n' Burger*, Murray Bridge, South Australia, 1995

John Werrett, *Fresh seafood restaurant*, Bairnsdale, Victoria, 1994

Brendan Bell, *Wash-house and laundromat*, Port Pirie, South Australia, 1997

Brendan Bell, *Drive-in bottle shop*, Port Lincoln, South Australia, 1997

Gordon Undy, *Facade of Jack & Newell building, Wharf Street*, Cairns, Queensland, 1995

Brendon Kelson, *Jewellers*, *Comur Street*, Yass, New South Wales, 1996

John Werrett, *Causeway kiosk*, Victor Harbor, South Australia, 1995

Reg Alder, *Supermarket*, Kununurra, Western Australia, 1994

Gordon Undy, *Fosseys*, Charters Towers, Queensland, 1996

Brendan Bell, *Shopping mall*, Dubbo, New South Wales, 1994

Grant Ellmers, *Radio Station 2WG, Fitzmaurice Street*, Wagga Wagga, New South Wales, 1996

Bob Miller, *The Northern Daily Leader office*, Tamworth, New South Wales, 1995

Aaron Bunch, *Miner bookshop/ABC centre*,
Kalgoorlie, Western Australia, 1995

LIVING

It is in Australia's homes that a recognisably Australian architecture emerges. Although most styles were borrowed, first from the British, and later from Europeans and Americans, they were transformed into something different because of the adaptations to design demanded by our climate and the adaptations to practice dictated by the availability of materials and infrastructure. As a result, our Victorian architecture is not just a good mimicry of what was happening in Britain at the time; it is some of the most impressive in the world.

Dotted around country Australia are old sandstone cottages with wrought-iron lace balustrades (p119), Spanish-influenced houses built between the world wars with ornamentation limited to the front porch (p112), ostentatious brick and Marseille-tiled houses built around Federation, featuring zinc-capped turrets and striking fretwork (p115)—sometimes only streets apart. This glorious meeting of styles is often not as lacking in cohesion as it might first seem; homes of wildly diverse architectural styles can be united by a common landscape and a strong sense of place. There are also often nods to topography in the architecture: glassed-in verandahs to protect against sea breezes; stilts or stumps to protect against flooding. The different styles within one town point to a sequence of economic and cultural development, and form an occasionally messy, occasionally incongruous, harmony.

Grant Ellmers, *'Fleetwood', 21 Gray Street*, Hamilton, Victoria, 1994

Grant Ellmers, *52 Coleman Street*, Wagga Wagga, New South Wales, 1996

Robert Deane, *260 Merri Street*, Warrnambool, Victoria, 1997

Joyce Evans, *House, Princes Street*, Burnie, Tasmania

Grant Ellmers, *126 Webster Street*, Ballarat, Victoria, 1994

Gordon Undy, *20 William Street*, East Maitland, New South Wales, 1995

Aaron Bunch, *House, Middleton Beach*, Albany, Western Australia, 1995

Peter Mathew, *House, Church Hill*, Gawler, South Australia, 1995

Robert Deane, *1 Victoria Street, cnr Edward Lane*, Mittagong, New South Wales, 1996

Aaron Bunch, *House, Spencer Street*, Albany, Western Australia, 1995

Bob Miller, *House, Auburn Vale Road*, Inverell, New South Wales, 1996

Mike Key, *52 Batchelor Street*, Queenstown, Tasmania, 1995

Robert Deane, *'Ierne', Spence Street*, Warrnambool, Victoria, 1997

Gordon Undy, *Pensioners' houses, bypass road*, Cloncurry, Queensland, 1996

Brendon Kelson, *Tiver's row, Truro Street*, Burra, South Australia, 1996

Gordon Undy, *Meatworkers' houses*, Rockhampton, Queensland, 1995

Bob Miller, *House, Jean Street*, Coffs Harbour, New South Wales, 1994

Raymond De Berquelle, *House, Davidson Street*, Deniliquin, New South Wales, 1994

Gordon Undy, *House, Mary Street*, Charters Towers, Queensland, 1996

Brendan Bell, *Lincoln Cove marina housing estate*, Port Lincoln, South Australia, 1997

PLAYING

Central to the life of country towns are those places we go to relax, move our bodies or socialise with friends. In this section are pubs, cinemas, cricket pavilions, pools, even an unlikely golf course in the northernmost town of the Kimberley (p153). Drive-ins began to appear in Australia in the 1950s and the Viewway (p140) opened halfway between Kalgoorlie and Boulder on 24 September 1958. The ticket office is a rather bland brick box, but the illuminated cursive sign announcing the 'Viewway' is all postwar pop art and rock and roll. Eighteen hundred kilometres north of the Viewway, the indomitable Sun Pictures (p141) in Broome has been entertaining locals for over 100 years. Once again it's the sign rather than the structure that does all the work here, screaming out to patrons with its jazz-age marquee bulb font.

As an island nation, leisure time is often connected with water, whether we live right next to it or as far away as you can get. Going to the beach has been a popular pastime since the mid-nineteenth century. This experience is often enhanced by the facilities (and icecream) available at bathing pavilions and surf clubs. Some, like the hundred-year-old pavilion (p158) in Austinmer, are historic buildings with local heritage significance. The suburban swimming pool could be just as architecturally interesting. Warwick's E.J. Portley Olympic Pool (p156) was built in 1957, when it was opened by state premier Frank Nicklin. Its striking curved brickwork entrance was demolished after this photo was taken. But it is preserved both in the memories of Warwick residents and in the National Library's collection.

Glenn Rees, *Railway hotel*, Gympie, Queensland, 1995

Reg Alder, *White Horse inn*, Berrima, New South Wales, 1994

Brendan Bell, *Great Northern hotel*, Newcastle, New South Wales, 1994

Raymond De Berquelle, *Hotel Terminus, North Street*, Shepparton, Victoria, 1994

Raymond de Berquelle, *Cock 'n' Bull restaurant, Warren Street*, Echuca, Victoria, 1994

Gordon Undy, *Barrier Reef hotel*, Cairns, Queensland, 1995

Aaron Bunch, *York hotel*, Kalgoorlie, Western Australia, 1995

Aaron Bunch, *'Viewway', drive-in cinema*, Kalgoorlie, Western Australia, 1995

Aaron Bunch, *Sun Pictures theatre*, Broome, Western Australia, 1995

Brendan Bell, *Australia cinema*, Orange, New South Wales, 1996

Mike Key, *Paragon theatre, McNamara Street*, Queenstown, Tasmania, 1995

THE
PARAGON
THEATRE
QUEENSTOWN INDOOR CRICKET

Mike Key, *Princess theatre, Brisbane Street*, Launceston, Tasmania, 1995

Brendan Bell, *Flinders theatre cinema*, Port Lincoln, South Australia, 1997

Brendan Bell, *Museum*, Bathurst, New South Wales, 1996

John Werrett, *Branch library, Kangaroo Flat*, Bendigo, Victoria, 1995

Glenn Rees, *Swimming pool, John Street*, Maryborough, Queensland, 1995

OLYMPIC SWIMMING
TOYOTA

Brendon Kelson, *Racecourse grandstand*, Tumut, New South Wales, 1996

Joyce Evans, *Football ground*, Burnie, Tasmania, 1995

Reg Alder, *Golf club*, Wyndham, Western Australia, 1994

Grant Ellmers, *Melville oval grandstand*, Hamilton, Victoria, 1994

Aaron Bunch, *Bowling club*, Geraldton, Western Australia, 1995

Mike Key, *Bowling club, cnr Ferry Street and Page Avenue*, New Norfolk, Tasmania, 1995

Glenn Rees, *E.J. Portley olympic pool, cnr Albert and Palmerin streets*, Warwick, Queensland, 1995

Mike Key, *North Esk rowing club*, Launceston, Tasmania, 1995

Angela Lynkushka, *Surf life saving club*, Austinmer, New South Wales, 1994

Brendan Bell, *Wharf*, Tathra, New South Wales, 1994

Published by National Library of Australia Publishing
Canberra ACT 2600
ISBN: 9781922507808

The National Library of Australia acknowledges Australia's First Nations Peoples—the First Australians—as the Traditional Owners and Custodians of this land and gives respect to the Elders—past and present—and through them to all Australian Aboriginal and Torres Strait Islander people.

Publisher: Lauren Smith
Managing editor: Amelia Hartney
Author and image curator: Matthew Jones
Designer: Hugh Ford
Image coordinator: Madeleine Warburton
Printed in China by The Australian Book Connection

The images in the Regional Cities and Major Towns project can be viewed on the National Library of Australia's catalogue at catalogue.nla.gov.au. Try searching by the name of the project, the name of a particular photographer or the name of a town. In some cases, the catalogue description contains further details about a building's history.

Find out more about NLA Publishing at nla.gov.au/national-library-publishing.

A catalogue record for this book is available from the National Library of Australia.